# The Upgrade

Look Your Best, Feel Your Best, Be Your Best!

**J.Renee**

authorHOUSE®

*AuthorHouse™*
*1663 Liberty Drive*
*Bloomington, IN 47403*
*www.authorhouse.com*
*Phone: 1 (800) 839-8640*

*Published by AuthorHouse    04/14/2015*

*ISBN: 978-1-5049-0699-9 (sc)*
*ISBN: 978-1-5049-0698-2 (e)*

*Library of Congress Control Number: 2015905798*

*Print information available on the last page.*

*Any people depicted in stock imagery provided by Thinkstock are models, and such images are being used for illustrative purposes only. Certain stock imagery © Thinkstock.*

*This book is printed on acid-free paper.*

## Dedication

To my late father, Pastor Raliegh A.
Jones Sr. you were my biggest fan.
Thank you for always pushing me
to maximize my potential.
Thank you for never letting me quit.
This book is for you.

# Acknowledgements

I would like to thank my family, friends, and clients for believing in me and lending your undying support. A special thank you also goes to Nakeia Daniels and The Writer's Fellowship Group for your skill and expertise in the production of this book. I couldn't have done it without you!

# Introduction

"NOPE! Not today. I'm *not* wearing pantyhose!"

I'll never forget the day I wrote my first song. I couldn't have been more than 12 years old, but I remember it like it was yesterday. It was a Sunday morning. Everyone was getting ready for church, and I was fully dressed (so I thought). I walked out of my room and headed towards the kitchen, but I didn't make it that far. My father immediately stopped me in the hall and asked, "Where are your pantyhose?" Of course this turned into an argument because I didn't want to wear any, and it ended in me sitting at the piano in the dining room, playing and singing the lyrics:

*"No pantyhose. No, I'm not wearing no panty hose."*

Growing up as the daughter of pastors and well-known community leaders, my siblings and I were raised to be examples. My parents understood that until we were of age, how we carried ourselves was ultimately a reflection of them. They couldn't control what we did and said as much as they probably wanted to, but as long as they were writing the checks, they were in control of what we wore and how we looked; and they made sure that we were presentable at all times.

Naturally, we resisted on every side. Although I enjoyed things like getting my hair done, I felt the rest of all that "girly stuff" my mom made me do and wear was totally unnecessary. I hated wearing dresses and pantyhose, as much as I'm sure my brothers hated wearing suits and ties. We saw it as torture, but what we didn't realize was that our parents were teaching us, and preparing us for the life that we were going to live as adults. It was that same *torture* that laid the foundation for the things I do for a living, as well as this book.

My resistance continued throughout my adolescent years. I didn't understand why all of the other kids got to wear jeans to church, but I had to wear dresses. I didn't understand why my parents were so adamant about my clothes fitting a certain way, and of course, I thought pantyhose were pointless. I reasoned that I should be able to wear all of the things that were cute and trendy; all of the things that the *other girls* were wearing, although my body was *all woman* by the age of 13. It was not until the latter years of high school that the light bulb came on.

Having an extensive background in music and performing arts, I was constantly on stages and in front of people. From pageantry to forensics, I was frequently in positions of judgment of both my talent, and my appearance. Even if I wasn't competing per se, I was often in positions where I was standing or speaking before people. I'm not sure exactly what caused me to have the epiphany, but at some point I began to realize that the way I looked could do one of two things: it could work for me, or it could work against me. It could help me accomplish my goal, or it could hinder my forward progress. My perception changed. I began looking closely at my peers, took notice of how they looked and what they were accomplishing as a result, and decided I wanted to be different.

I didn't know where exactly I was going to end up, or what I was going to be doing, but I knew I was destined for something great, and I knew that my life was going to be a source of inspiration for many people. Consequently, I knew that if I wanted more for my life, and if I wanted to be better, then my appearance was going to have to reflect that. It was then that I began to transition my image from that of the teenage girl that I was, to the professional, sophisticated woman I wanted to be. I wrote down exactly what I wanted to look like and the image I wanted to portray. I then purged my closet, and made a list of things that I felt I needed in my wardrobe. It was way too much to purchase at once, so I separated it into three stages based off of importance, and by the time I was done with all three stages I looked like a new woman. I was carrying myself as if I had already reached my destination; as though I was driving a Benz, not my mom's old mini-van. Eventually, others began to take notice, and began reaching out to me for help. I used the same step-by-step process I took myself through on other people, and they began to see results. Inspired by Beyoncé's hit song, I coined this transformative process The Upgrade.

I knew that everyone was not as image-conscious as I had become, but I presumed that most of us had a little common sense when it came to the basics of being a woman. As time passed, and I transitioned from being a teenager, to a college student, to becoming an image consultant and professional hair and makeup artist, I was able to meet many women from a wide variety of backgrounds - most of which were not like mine. I began to notice a recurring theme with women young and old: many had never been educated on or exposed to the fundamentals of how to dress and/or carry themselves appropriately based on the occasion. Moreover, as I continued my career in the beauty industry I encountered more and more women that were hurting because they really did not like the way they looked.

Every time I met a hurting soul, or saw a tear fall, my heart broke for the women that could not look in the mirror and smile at what was looking back at them. The more I watched and studied these hurting souls, I began to realize that there was a story behind every tear. There was a story behind every short skirt and every unkempt head of hair. I learned of countless stories - motherless homes, life changing tragedies that caused both physical and emotional damage, to being in relationships and marriages with men that drained their self-esteem. What I was discovering was that everybody has a story, and many times we'd rather push our issues under the rug, or put a bandage over them than actually deal with the root of the problem. Realizing how much the mental and emotional state of a woman affects her physical appearance is what inspired me to write this book. I want to open up "Pandora's box" and deal with the root of the issue, so that you, the reader, can make a permanent change that resonates on both the inside and outside. It is my desire for this book to ignite a fire that causes a total transformation, from the inside, out.

This book was not written to address style; nor was this book written for the divas or self-proclaimed *fashionistas*. This book was written for real women with real issues: Women honest enough to admit that they want to make a change. Some of our greatest issues as women are centered on the way we look and the way that we *feel* about the way that we look. It is a problem I know that I was called to help solve. Whether you are a teenager on the brink of womanhood, or an adult woman looking to refine your image, I believe that The Upgrade will be an insightful read for you. I hope you enjoy reading it as much as I enjoyed writing it.

*The Upgrade*

# Chapter 1

## *Imaging on Purpose*

Take a moment and look at yourself in the mirror. I mean *really* look. Give yourself a good once over. Look at your hair, your makeup, your jewelry, or the lack thereof, and the clothes that you have on. Honestly, do you like the way you look? If not, why don't you like the way you look? Moreover, why do you look the way you look? What were you thinking when you got dressed this morning – or were you even thinking at all? What message are you relaying? Is it the message that you want to send? More importantly, do you think your image is helping you, or hurting you?

Whether it is conscious or subconscious, there is indeed a psychological explanation as to why you look the way you look. In this chapter, we will discuss what is going on inside that is making you look the way you look on the outside. Don't worry, I am not a psychologist, so I'm not going to give you a clinical diagnosis. However, I will be sharing many of the issues I have encountered with the numerous women I have helped over the years, and hopefully give you the insight needed to understand something I call **Imaging On Purpose**.

஭ ௐ

Physical appearance is probably one of the greatest roots of insecurity in women. As if the societal pressures of perfection aren't enough, our images are under constant criticism and scrutiny from friends, family, and even our mates. If we gain weight, change our hair or our style, whether we like it or not everyone is going to have an opinion. People won't always tell you when you they think you look good, but they always seem to find a way to let you know when they think you look bad. No one wants to deal with negative criticism in an area as sensitive as physical appearance, so in efforts to avoid that, often times we find ourselves conforming to please others, or worse, not putting forth any effort because we don't want to be noticed at all. Conforming is not merely doing what others would approve of, it can also mean *not* doing things that would risk disapproval or blending in the crowd to avoid being noticed either way.

I believe the pressure to please others is the reason why so many of us are confused and insecure about the way we look. The reality is everyone can appreciate a sincere compliment; we all enjoy knowing that our appearance is attractive, even if only to your significant other. It would be misleading if I portrayed myself to be a super woman who is an exception to the rule. I enjoy a sincere compliment the same as everyone else.

However, the day I discovered the utopian pleasure of self-satisfaction, my life changed. That was the day I accepted my body and size for being what it is, not what I imagined it to be. It was the day I realized that my destiny could ultimately be hindered not only by the way I look, but the way I *feel* about myself. It was the day I discovered that even though I was not currently pleased with the way I looked, I had all the power I needed to change myself. It was then that I realized that I could do it, and so can you.

I discovered that I couldn't do what everyone else does, or wear what everyone else wears. That day I learned to please the woman in the mirror, rather than looking to others for affirmation. I found out that if I learned to love and care for myself, it would become a revolving gift, blessing me internally, and as a bonus, showing the world who I really am.

That day I realized that I shouldn't have to work for my image. It should work for me. That day I discovered the power of ***Imaging On Purpose.***

ℰℭ

Now, you're probably wondering what purpose has to do with the way you look. Let me assure you, purpose has everything to do with the way you look. Just as every day should be lived with purpose, you should get dressed, do your hair, and your makeup (if you wear it) on a daily basis with a purpose in mind. Ask yourself, "What do I want to accomplish today? And how will my image help or hurt me?"

These are questions that many people do not ask themselves on a daily basis. However, when you understand the correlation between who you are, your purpose, your image, and your personal brand, ***Imaging On Purpose*** becomes second nature. Lack of intention leaves too much room for assumption. We are women. Everything we do should be done on purpose.

ഇ෬

### Steps to Understanding Imaging On Purpose

#### WHO AM I?

Having a realistic understanding and acceptance of who you are is essential in The Upgrade. If we're honest, we are all guilty of envying the life of someone else at some point. There is no denying it. However, in reality we will never be able to have someone else's life, nor will we ever be able to look the way someone else looks. You can emulate and try to recreate all you want, but your job is your job, your body is your body, and your life is your life. I harp on this point because so many women get caught up in trying to be like someone else or trying to live someone else's life, but their failed attempts can be painfully obvious and embarrassing.

Who you are is not just the way you look; it is your lifestyle, your personality, the things you love, the things you hate, what you believe in - all these things encompass who you are. Many of your personal attributes are visible in your physical appearance, which is the reason you can't waste time pretending to be anyone else. It's a temporary fix and just won't be enough when you're looking for lasting change.

It may seem simple, but having a pure and accurate understanding of who you are is the first, and for many the hardest step in the process of ***Imaging On Purpose***. Maybe your issue isn't that you're trying to look like someone else. Your problem might be that you are stuck looking like someone you were; someone that was supposed to be a "transitional" you, not a "permanent" you. Regardless of what your situation may be, you need to come to an accurate understanding of who you are, so that you focus on who you will become. Establish who you are, what you are, and what you want to represent. Then, and only then, will you be ready to move forward in the process of image reformation.

We all experience different stages in life, and often times the mental transition out of these stages proves to be far easier than the physical transition. Which brings me to my next question.

**WHERE AM I?**

I am not talking about your actual location at this moment. This questions refers to where you are in life. What stage of life are you in? Where is your focus at this point in life? What are your current resources? Ask yourself, "Why am I here? Am I here by choice? If so, what is supposed to be accomplished in this particular season of my life?"

Being able to accurately identify where you are in life is necessary in planning for where you are going. Although this book is about upgrading and moving from where you are into something greater, you have to be realistic about the current state of your life and your current resources. I am a firm believer in looking like where you are going rather than where you are, but it is still very important to be cognizant and sensitive to your current environment and stage of life. Although every woman is different, we all go through the similar if not some of the same stages of life, and every woman reaches that season where it takes a little more push and drive to move into the next stage of life. See if you can find yourself stuck in any of these stages:

1) The Grasshopper - The grasshopper, or adolescent stage is probably the most unstable and inconsistent stage of all of the stages that you will experience in life, but fortunately there is absolutely nothing wrong with it. It is the stage in which we are introduced to the world; the stage that we begin to figure out what life is really about.

This stage typically comes right after high school or for many, the beginning years of college. You are still young and naïve, yet thrust into a world where being a girl is no longer acceptable; you must be a woman to survive. It is during this time that you begin to try new things and to form your own opinions. Physically, your body begins to go through changes. The infamous "freshman 15" and/or post high school weight gain sets in, and your skin also begins to change. In this stage of life your mind and body both change as a result of a drastic change of lifestyle, and naturally your image follows suit. For the first time, your image is no longer under the tight thumb of your mother or maternal figure. You can wear what you want, when you want, and how you want. You can do what you want to your hair- you can essentially do whatever you want. You are still trying to figure out what you want from life, so you may try, do, say, and wear your most controversial items during this time. You don't really have a consistent job or career, so your professional image is of no concern to you. In this stage everything your mother taught you will be tested, or everything your mother didn't teach you will show. It was this time of trial and error really that inspired me to write this book. I can remember the thrill of walking out of my dorm in something I know my mother would disapprove of, only to later go back to my room and change. A time of growth, change, and experimentation: There is nothing wrong with being the grasshopper. The only problem is staying a grasshopper. Then you become what I like to call:

2) The Right Now Woman - The Right Now stage is where many women get stuck; living for now, dressing for now, with no concern for the future. This is the stage that usually comes with the self-certification of being grown. In Beyoncé's song "Grown Woman" she boldly proclaims that because she is grown, she can do what she wants, and that's exactly how we feel during this stage. We are no longer the scared grasshopper, but we aren't quite the mature woman yet.

Many adapt the "YOLO", "I don't care", "living for the moment" mentality as a coping mechanism. We don't really know where we are going, we don't know what we want to do with our lives, nor do we have a legitimate plan for the future, so all of our effort and energy goes into living for Right Now. This is the woman that is still partying when her friends have stopped, the woman that is still in school while most of her peers have graduated; the woman that has changed her major and career goals countless times with no end in sight.

As it pertains to image: this is the woman that has tons of dresses to wear to the club, but she struggles to dress appropriately for a job interview. This is the woman that owns countless pairs of tennis shoes, but doesn't own a basic pair of black pumps. This is the woman that has jeans and t-shirts aplenty, but doesn't have anything she can wear to church. This stage knows no particular age bracket because sadly enough, many women come into this stage very young and never grow out of it. Because of this, the Right Now woman always struggles with the way she looks. She is never truly satisfied with who she sees in the mirror because overall, she is not satisfied with her life.

Change in life is inevitable, and as you get older, more will be required of you as a woman. At some point you will be forced to go beyond your Right Now environment, and you need to be prepared to dress and carry yourself accordingly. You may not need a skirt of decent length because you don't go to church now, but at some point in your life you may have to attend a church function. You may be wearing a uniform at the minimum wage job you're working now, but at some point you will need professional attire to wear to an interview. You may not see the need to have a nice cocktail dress now, but at some point you will have to attend a wedding or a formal event. The Right Now woman does not think about these things, therefore she doesn't feel the need to invest in anything beyond her Right Now.

3) The Career Woman – Every career driven woman comes to the stage in her journey where life must take a back seat, and career must take the front seat. There is no career that will not require some sort of sacrifice, and if you want a career of any type of substance at some point its establishment and maintenance will have to be top priority. The Career Woman adjusts her everyday living around her job, or the pursuit of her job and its requirements, especially if she works a lot. It is totally natural to conform our daily image and wardrobe to our 9-5 environment. However, many women get so engulfed in their career and the image it requires that they struggle dressing outside of the workplace. Whether you work in a corporate environment where the standard is business professional attire or you work in a casual environment where you wear scrubs and tennis shoes as your uniform, it is important to have balance and versatility in your image. Often times the image struggle in this stage is far deeper than simply buying clothes that can be worn outside of work; many

women can't dress aside from work attire because they don't have a life outside of work. They lack balance: They don't have a social life, nor are they apart of anything else that requires versatility, so when those rare occasions arise when they have to step outside of the norm, they may struggle. Of all of the stages, this is probably the only stage that women get stuck in by choice.

Many use career as an escape from life. We are all, or will all be guilty of this at some point. We try to channel frustration and dissatisfaction with our personal lives into drive and motivation to work, and theoretically, that's not always a bad thing. It becomes a problem when it becomes a way of life, and we refuse to deal with the root of our issues. Just as that can be detrimental for our emotional and mental health, it can be just as detrimental for our image and physical presentation. Your confidence and drive should show in your everyday presentation, not just when you are going to work.

On the flip side, some people are stifled by their work environment. If your work environment does not require you to maintain a certain image, it is easy to become sluggish and find yourself "putting on" only when you think people are looking. However, the fact of the matter is that people are always looking, and they decide how they feel about you and what you have to offer before you ever open your mouth or present a resume.

4) The Mommy/Family Woman – Now let's talk about Mommies. This is probably the most obvious stage to identify because it is so typical, and it is so very noticeable. We have all seen it. We all have a friend or maybe we are the woman that: 1) gives birth and loses your life and livelihood in your child/ children, 2) gained baby weight that you can't seem to lose and as a result of a lack of confidence and lowered self-esteem you begin to let yourself go. Both scenarios are tragic and yet both are unbelievably common.

Let me give this disclaimer: I firmly believe that there is no greater responsibility than that of rearing a child, and your children should be of the utmost priority. There are indeed some sacrifices, whether it be time or money, sleep or privacy that must be made in order to secure a stable life for your child or children. However, you cannot surrender your purpose, identity, and existence as a woman just to become a mother. Even if you put your life on hold for a while, don't forget it altogether.

While that may sound harsh, you wouldn't surrender your social security number when you give birth and take on that of your child's, likewise your physical identity remains even after motherhood begins. Just as you had a life prior to the birth of your child, it is only a matter of time before the child grows up and begins to develop a life of his or her own. The will beg and plead for their identity to be detached from yours, so you have to be willing to detach yours from theirs. Invest in their life by all means, but please, don't forget about your own. Being overly consumed in the "mommy" role can not only effect your life, but it could potentially begin to effect your relationships; the major one being your marriage.

What about dating and marriage? The wife/significant other role is probably just as sensitive to talk about as the motherhood is. As women, we are natural caregivers and have a natural desire to please. We want our mates to be pleased with our appearance, but often times we lose ourselves in our efforts to satisfy. Although I do believe there should be a certain level of consideration for your husband's desires, you can never lose sight of who you should ultimately aim to please, and that is yourself.

Your significant other can tell you every day that you look amazing, but if you don't like what you see, you will never be satisfied, even if they are. They may not admit it, but men actually appreciate the confidence we exude when we are pleased with ourselves. I would even go as far as to say men enjoy a woman that has the "Take it, or leave it" mentality. He wants to know that you are willing to negotiate in some areas, but a man will appreciate a woman that is confident in who she is and what she has to offer; confident enough not to compromise who she is for him or anyone else. While this may sound selfish, it's really the highest form of appreciation for who God made us. It isn't selfish when you walk in your purpose. It's natural and lovely and pure. Anyone worth having in your life will recognize this not as vanity, but as appreciation for the gift God that is you.

They have to be made to understand that when they commit to being with you it is a commitment to everything that you are; the good, the bad, the things they like and the things they don't like. Whether you want to add some pizazz to your wardrobe or if you want to change your hair, you need room within a relationship to be able to grow and change while at the same time respecting your mate in the process.

Sadly enough, you may not be given that leverage unless you demand it. That won't come from stomping your foot and yelling "I'M GROWN! I CAN DO WHAT I WANT! It won't come from throwing tantrums or using manipulation. It comes by simply being the strong woman you know you are and displaying your individual confidence naturally. Whether you are single or married, whether you have 5 children or no children; never lose sight of who you are.

5) The Wonder Years Woman - The Wonder Years Woman or the, *I remember when* woman, is typically a woman that has gotten older and set in her ways. This stage doesn't necessarily have to come when you are "old", it can come at any time after you have lived through one or more of the other stages. This is the stage that often comes after you're settled and established. Life has slowed down a lot, and so have you. You're not going as much as you used to go, nor are you doing as much as you used to do, and it usually begins to show in the way that you look. This stage often shows through physical weight gain, or just an overall decline in your personal appearance. Or it may not be that you look unkempt - it might be that you just look the same way you've looked for years; stuck in a time warp. You have been where you are for so long that you have lost your desire for growth and change. You are comfortable with your life, your same hair style, your same wardrobe, you are comfortable with your job, your personal life - you are comfortable with things staying the same. You may not necessarily like where

you are or how you look, but you're not motivated to make a change. You can reach this point at 25, or 45. This stage knows no particular age. This could be the woman that has been wearing the same clothes for the last 10 years, or this could be the woman that looks at younger women or older pictures of themselves and says "I remember when..."

Human nature says go for what you know, and run from what you don't. It is that risk-free mentality that keeps us stuck in a crippling, stifling, box. Many women feel that after a certain age they're too old to wear certain things or dress themselves up, and there is some merit to that. However, you're never too old to invest in yourself. Be honest with yourself... are you truly happy with how you look and how I feel? If the answer is no, I have some good news and some bad news for you. The good news is that as long as you are living and breathing you have the opportunity to change that. However, the bad news is that change will not happen unless you make it happen. You're constantly growing and changing, and your image should grow and evolve as you do.

Whether you find yourself stuck in any of those particular stages (maybe you found a little bit of you in each stage), you are an excellent candidate for The Upgrade. I assume that you are reading this book because you have the desire to change, or the desire to improve, and this is an excellent start. Fully understanding where you are and who you are, will help you understand why you are.

If you are a young med-school student focused on graduation that might explain why your closet is full of jeans, scrubs, and tennis shoes, and why you don't take much time to spruce yourself up. If you are still trying to find yourself and in the process are experimenting with the Right Now lifestyle until you discover your path that might explain why your day-to-day appearance is inconsistent with who you really are. If you are a single mother and work full time, that clearly explains why neither your hair or nails are a major priority, and why you may not put the little free time and energy you have into your appearance.

Are you seeing the correlation?

This brings us to the most important question of them all:

Ask yourself, where am I going?

## WHERE AM I GOING?

This is a simple question with a not-so-simple answer. Many people struggle with life in its entirety just because they cannot answer this question. The answer to the question is especially important in the process. Where do you see yourself in two years? How about five years from now? You may be living comfortably or even thriving in a particular industry right now, but where do you want to end up? You may be a jobless college grad right now, but what job are you looking for? You want to be an entrepreneur, but what business do you plan on starting exactly?

Commonly enough, many women do not look the way they want to look right now because they are not where they want to be in life, and they don't feel motivated to do or be more. Here's the truth: You can't change how you look in your current state if you have no idea where you want to be or how you are going to get there. When you travel, most of the time you pack before you leave home with your destination in mind. Often times we reach our destinations and realize that we are not as prepared as we should be, and as a result of poor planning and packing, we have to pay the high cost of inconvenience to get what we need after the fact. The same principle holds true with your image. You can't wait until you are an attorney to buy your first suit. You must know that you want to be an attorney before you can begin to prepare for that position. Once you know you want to be an attorney, start planning from that moment.

My life changed the day I decided that I was going to stop dressing for the girl that I was at that moment, and start dressing for the business woman I was going to be. I was 16 years old when the shift began to take place. Before that time in my life, I was all over the place. From the tom-boy look, to the ghetto-princess look (I'll leave that to your imagination). I tried it all. Nothing I tried felt comfortable for me because I knew I wasn't being myself. As I neared the end of high school, I began to really think and pray about the woman I wanted to be. I knew that I wanted to be able to touch people and change lives, I knew I wanted to be respected, and I knew that I wanted to be a business owner. I didn't know how all of that was going to come together, but I knew I couldn't achieve those things looking like everybody else.

From the moment I began to make the change, I was criticized by my peers. I was told I was dressing like a white girl because most of the black girls in my school didn't dress the way I was dressing nor did they carry themselves in the way that I was aspiring to carry myself. (Ironically, staying to true to myself through all the criticism paid off because those same people that talked about me where the ones that turned around and voted me best dressed. Go figure.) But I knew I wasn't meant to live an average life, and that I was meant to be set apart. From the moment of that epiphany I began to carry myself like I was the entrepreneur I am today. I knew where I wanted to end up, and how I wanted to be viewed, so I made sure everything about my image intentionally supported that. I began ***Imaging On Purpose.***

Here's another truth. As much as we want to stress the fact that inner beauty is what really counts, and truly it does, we cannot ignore the fact that 50-70% of communication is physical. People decide how they feel about you, your services, and your professionalism fundamentally off of their initial perception of how you look/present yourself. Knowing that, why wouldn't you carry yourself in a way that would display your anticipation and readiness for your bright future?

Understanding is key in making changes that will endure. Now that we have gotten that out of the way, let's move deeper into the process.

# Chapter 2

## *Right for You vs. Wrong for You*

Is your current image helping or hurting your purpose? Is the way you look an accurate reflection of who you are and what you represent? What kind of attention are you attracting with your current physical presentation?

As an image consultant, these were some of the first questions I asked my clients when they would tell me of their interest in image reformation. As we get deeper into the psychological aspect of why you look the way you look and how it affects your day-to-day life, you will need to be honest yourself and answer these questions. Even if you are unsure about where you are going, use your current circumstances as a reference point.

Is the way you look right now helping or hurting you? Is it a place of satisfaction or point of stress? Are you comfortable with your image? Is it making you more productive on your job? Is it keeping the spice in your marriage? If your answer to any of these questions is coupled with a negative connotation, what is keeping you from making the changes you need to make? The beautiful part about being unhappy with the way we look is that we ultimately possess that power to change it. Think about your image as if it were a house.

When you walk into someone's house you can tell a lot about who they are as a person, and what is important to them. You can always tell when someone is innovative and embraces change, because their house will reflect innovation and change. My mother is a great example of that. Over the course of the last 20 years, the house I grew up in has been painted more times than I can count, bathrooms have been added, the deck has been replaced, furniture has come and gone, and all the floors have been changed, even multiple times in some places in the house. The house was built in the 70's but you would never know because it looks modern now. As times have changed, the house has changed with it, to the point that the house is worth a substantial amount more than what it was initially purchased for.

When you walk into my childhood home you can tell much about my mother based on what she has done within the walls.

On the contrary, you can walk into a similar style home down the street, and have a drastically different experience. If it is the home of someone who is more set in their ways, and does not embrace change, often times they have the same furniture they have had for years. The same paint and wall paper that was there when they moved in is still up. The house smells and looks old and outdated, and would not be very appealing for someone else to purchase. The same exact model, with the same square footage, built in the same year might sell for far less because of the simple fact the presentation is the not the best. Some of the first things that realtors suggest when someone is interested in selling a home is making sure that everything that is broken or not working properly is fixed, thoroughly cleaning the house so that it looks and smells nice, and modernizing the house so that it can be more appealing in the current competitive market.

Those same standards apply to your image. In order to continue to be a viable and competitive force in today's world both personally and professionally, you cannot allow yourself to get trapped in the "if it ain't broke, don't fix it" mentality! Don't wait until your hair to starts to turn gray before you add a little color! Don't wait until your marriage is failing to try to start sprucing yourself up! Be the best you can be now and at all times. If you're not interested in ever moving beyond where you are, or even capitalizing on your current circumstances, then you can close this book right now. However, if you want to continue to grow and evolve, not only must you embrace change, but you must initiate it!

ℰℭ

In the previous chapter we discussed ***Imaging On Purpose***, and the importance of knowing who you are, where you are, and where you are going. Those things are fundamental in this process. Now that we understand the correlation between your purpose and your image, we can go deeper into the psychological aspect of why you look the way you look, then help you understand what is right for you versus what is wrong for you.

Now, be honest. Do you really like the way you look? If you struggle with the issue of right versus wrong regarding your image you may have a deeper issue, which is ultimately an overall dissatisfaction with who you are. Eventually that dissatisfaction leads to denial, which leads to confusion, which leads to a bad case of WRONG!

Body image is definitely the greatest root of dissatisfaction in terms of overall image in women. We live in a day and time when media exploitation is at an all-time high. As if the outdated shackles of the 36-24-36 "standard" isn't enough, we have constant reminders through social media, television, and magazines of what "perfection" is supposed to look like. Whereas at one point in time our differences were embraced as defining factors that made us unique, now a little shot here and a little surgery there can have anyone living in their dream body. Dieting, and get slim quick schemes are trending like never before, making everyone give their body a second look.

I am a supporter of healthy living and being in the best possible shape you can be in. However, we have to be real with ourselves, you may want to look different or to be shaped differently but your desire doesn't change what is fact, and you have to carry yourself accordingly.

Being in denial about who you are and wearing things that don't fit or accentuate your positives will not make you look any better. Yes, you will get attention, but it won't be the kind of attention that you want. The same applies with your hair and makeup. Everyone wants to be hip and contemporary, however you have to do what works for you; put your own spin on what is current. Every person has something about their body that they don't necessarily love, you just have to learn how to carry yourself in a way that would accentuate the positives. However, if you are unhappy with your size there is absolutely nothing wrong in taking steps to becoming a better and healthier you.

So let's get down to the black and white. How do you know what is right or wrong for you and your body type? Every shape is different, but there are some general rules for each basic body type that will ensure you look your best.

&#x20AC;&#x20AC;

**Hair and Makeup (my favorite topic!)**

When it comes down to your hair, I always suggest to think opposite. What I mean by that is there are certain components that are already present in your natural state of existence. The way to compliment them would be by presenting a contrasting style or color. For example: If you have a round face, a bold hair cut with strong lines would look great on you, whereas a more round cut would cause your face to look even more round. On the contrary, if you have stronger lines in your face and more defined features, a softer cut would be more fitting. As for color, why do you think so many women with darker skin look great with blonde hair, women that are fair skinned look amazing with dark hair, and women with olive/ yellow tones in their skin look great with red hair? Because of the contrasting tones! Hair color can be tricky, but I believe that there is a hue for everyone. It's all about connecting the tone that compliments your skin the best. After all, your hair is your greatest accessory, so have fun with it! Cut it off, color it, add extensions – have fun! As long as you are using professional services and keeping your hair healthy in the process, do whatever you feel bold enough to do.

The only thing trickier than hair color, is makeup. There are so many rules and theories as to who can wear what in makeup it can be intimidating. Yes, some colors look better on certain skin tones and facial structures, but I don't believe any color rules in makeup are indisputable. The trick to being able to pull of any color is always anchoring that color with another color close to or in the family of your skin tone. For example, I have full lips, but I love bold lipstick. To avoid the look I don't want, often times I will apply a brown, flesh toned lip liner before applying the lipstick. This slightly darkens the color around the perimeter of my lips so there isn't such a harsh line of demarcation, which keeps the definition I want around the edges of my lips. If you are wearing a bright color on your eyes, using a similar, flesh toned or slightly darker crease color will balance out the brightness. It's that simple. Now let's move into an area that is a little more complicated.

## DRESSING YOUR BODY TYPE
### Slender Build

Most would think that the smaller you are, the easier it is to dress your body, but dressing a slender body can prove to be just as challenging as dressing a large body. You want to avoid extremely tight clothing at all costs, especially if you are slim to the point that your bones are protruding or abnormally visible. You want your clothing to fit, however, you want to lean towards clothing that gives you shape. For example, a tailored, fitted dress made of a stronger fabric would complement your body structure better than a clingy, jersey-knit dress. Also, the concept of body balance will always work in your favor. A lose top and a fitted bottom, or vice versa, will create the appearance of a little more depth in your frame.

### Hips Don't Lie

Now we all know a bottom-heavy, hippy woman that doesn't seem to get it (maybe you *are* that woman). Although having a thicker lower half is trending and popular right now, you still don't want to do or wear things that will draw too much attention to that area. The fact of the matter is if it's there, it will be seen regardless, even if you have on a trash bag. There is no need to wear things that will draw excessive attention to that area. Bottoms that are cut straight are most complimentary for this particular body type. Bottoms that narrow or even bell at the bottom can make you look even larger, but a straight cut will do the trick. Also, more structured, fitted (not tight) tops will synch your waistline and give the appearance of an hour glass rather than a wide load.

### Boxes and Such

Those who have a "boxier" frame have a little more work to do, but don't be nervous. I've got you covered. A box frame can be large or small - it is a frame that is straight up and down, or lacks the contours of our *hippy* sisters. In this instance you have to create the lines and curves you want to see. High wasted belts, empire-waist dresses, bell sleeved tops, skinny or narrow cut pants, and A-line skirts will all be your friends. Why? Because they all add shape. If you're going for a curvy look you'll want to avoid anything that is cut straight or lacks shape because it will only accentuate your "box" shape.

### BUSTing at the Seams

This can be one of the hardest, if not the hardest body type to dress. Being "busty" or having large breasts (to be politically correct), can be extremely frustrating, especially if they are not in proportion to the rest of your body. This area of the body seems to effect self-esteem the most; either in the sense that a woman is very self-conscious about this area, or in the sense that she tries to exploit this area for attention. It is indeed a struggle, however, in the event that you cannot change your size, you have to do what you can to make the best of the situation. If you're already busty, you never want to wear things that will draw excessive attention to your breasts, or make them look even larger. Take advantage of structured tops and dresses. Go for things that are narrowed at the waist but suitable to your breast size to create a more balanced look. Anything that is narrow all the way down will only make your top half look larger. You may also want to find a great seamstress or tailor that can adjust and take in clothing that you have to buy in a larger size to fit your breast.

Getting dressed can be frustrating, but it is especially frustrating when you are dressing a body that you are not satisfied with. Everyone has something that they would like to change about their body, and there is nothing wrong with taking steps to becoming a better you. Work out, eat healthy, drop a few pounds here, tone up there; there is nothing wrong with that. Change the things that you can, and learn to accept the things that you cannot change. Have limits and boundaries, and know that imperfections are what makes each of us beautiful!

## Marital Status

What on earth does marital status have to do with the way that you look? Marital Status has EVERYTHING to do with the way you look! We have all heard some of the traditional sayings and standards of how a *married woman* should look, or things that only *single women* do. I will never forget it. I was a freshman at Tennessee State University, and one Sunday I decided to wear some elaborately designed fishnet tights to church. I was not dressed inappropriately by any means, and the tights were not revealing at all, however the church that I was visiting that Sunday was a more conservative church.

One of the Elders' wives came up to me and told me how gorgeous my tights were, and how she wished she could wear tights like that but she was too old. As I prepared to respond, our conversation was cut short as her husband swept into the conversation and said, "Those are the kinds of tights single women wear". We all laughed, but I was extremely uncomfortable with his statement. I was totally taken aback. I had never heard anyone say anything like that, especially not to me. But the reality is a lot of people think that way, and although that may have been a little drastic, there is actually some merit to that theory. I am not suggesting that married women walk around looking like nuns, but I am suggesting that a married woman should carry herself differently than a woman who is single and looking to be found.

**All the Single Ladies!**

Let's get this straight now: If you're not married, you're single. When you fill out official documents they ask you if you are married, single, divorced, or widowed. There is no box for "in a relationship". Until he "puts a ring on it" or is on the brink of putting a ring on it, you are SINGLE and there is no obligation for you to adjust who you are or how you look to please a man.

Just putting that out there.

And even AFTER he puts a ring on it, you still...... Well... that's another book. Let's talk single women!

There is indeed something very liberating about being single. You can do what you want, and be who you want, whenever you want. It is indeed a time in life that should be cherished and enjoyed. If you are single and you don't desire companionship or to be married, then keep doing whatever you want! However, if you desire companionship, there should be some thought and conscious effort that goes into your physical presentation.

Disclaimer: I do not believe in doing ANYTHING simply to please a man, or to snag yourself a man and this is not what I am suggesting by any stroke of the imagination. Think about it like this: one of the signature pleasures of buying a new car is the new car scent. It is unmatchable. Even though there are tons of car fresheners that claim to have the "new car scent", nothing smells like a new car. When you first purchase the car, you are constantly cleaning it and doing whatever you can to keep that scent alive. We all know that eventually that scent will fade, it's inevitable. Nevertheless, no one wants to buy a new car that smells like an old car, even it if is used! Your initial presentation to the world as a single woman is that new car scent!

Most couples that have been together for any length of time have grown and changed, and neither of the two people look the same way they did when they got together. Yet you can almost guarantee if you were to ask either of them "At what point was your mate the most attractive to you?" and they answered honestly, their answer would be "when we first met". Why? It's that NEW CAR SCENT! You always want to put your best foot forward, especially when you are interested in getting off the lot. Furthermore, you don't want to be sold for any old price - you want to be sold to the highest bidder, figuratively speaking of course. In order for that to happen you want to make sure that everything is in tip-top "selling condition". Wear and tear over time is normal and inevitable, but nobody wants to buy the car already beat up and tore down! In the event that someone does purchase a car in that state it is always a last resort, or something that is done out of desperation. Those types of situations never last and even when they do, they can be full of misery and neglect.

It's only a matter of time before they become disgusted with the old, beat down car, and trade it in for something better. That is not the type of buyer you want for your car is it? Be the best you can be so that you can attract the best mate for you. Yes, the inner woman is the most important, but the outer woman is who will be seen first. She is who will provoke the initial attraction. The beautiful thing about that is many of the attributes of the inner woman can be shown through the outer woman. With that being said, you want to make sure that your outer woman is an accurate reflection of who you are, and what you represent.

A woman's morals, standards, and values are all visible in the way that she carries herself. Don't forsake the things that essentially make you who you are to attract a man. You are looking for Mr. Right, not Mr. Right Now. Mr. Right is attracted to a woman that keeps herself up, not a woman that dresses just to get attention. Mr. Right is attracted to a woman who is contemporary and allows her best assets to shine, yet understands the importance of Victoria still having some "secrets", if you get my meaning. Mr. Right will appreciate a woman who takes pride in her appearance, but is not so self-consumed that she is in the mirror taking pictures all day, every day.

On the contrary, Mr. Right Now is attracted to the woman that puts on a show. He's attracted to a woman who has a lustful appeal - the woman who gets all the "likes" on Instagram. Mr. Right Now doesn't care about who you are, where you are going, or how he can complement you in that process. Mr. Right Now just wants what he can get from you. He wants to drive that new car until that scent wears off, then he wants to take you back to the dealership so that he can take another new car for a spin. Or who knows, he might not take you back to the dealership, he might just get another car and take turns driving both.

Either way, Mr. Right Now will never be the man of your dreams. It is so hard to uphold the standard of class in a day and time where sexual exploitation rules, and dominates everything we see. However, even Mr. Right Now will eventually grow and mature to the point that he doesn't want a "Right Now" girl anymore. Classiness always wins. You are what you attract, and you will attract what you are. Be the best. Attract the best.

### So He Put a Ring On It...

Congratulations to you! Many wanted the opportunity but you are one! I guess now that you have your husband the hard part is over, so you can just kick your feet up and cruise right?

Wrong.

This is a common mistake that I have witnessed some married women make: They present one image in the dating phase that provokes the initial attraction, then they get married, get too busy or worse, lazy, and let themselves go. This can be part of the cause of many problems in marriages because women become too dependent on the love that is or should be based off of non-physical things, and they think that it is strong enough to cover and make their husband totally oblivious to their physical woes.

Granted, that love should be strong enough to cover all physical imperfections, however, the only way to totally ignore the physical aspect of the relationship is if both people are either not human or blind. As long as your husband has eyes to see, he can see when you're not at your best! He can see when you're not happy with yourself, and he can also FEEL when you're not happy with yourself. Now even in the case of marriage I still believe that your ultimate goal should be to satisfy the woman in the mirror. I don't think I can emphasize that point enough. Because when you do it for you, you'll never lose.

Whether you're noticed or not won't matter as much because you'll be happy with yourself. That kind of joy is contagious and spills over into other areas of your life.

Ironically, many men idolize celebrities that are glammed out from head to toe with weave down their back and enough makeup on for a circus show, but they will say they want a plain-Jane woman with a basic wardrobe that wears her real hair and doesn't wear any makeup at all. Take the things that he likes into consideration, but at the end of the day do what truly makes you happy. This is why it is so important to be who you are from start to finish, from the first date, to the altar. I wasn't trying to be funny when I said if you're not married, you're single, and that you shouldn't be altering who you are to please a man during the dating phase.

If he can control how you look then, he will control how you look for the rest of your life and you may come to resent him for doing something you allowed in the first place. If you present an honest image of who you are and what you like from the beginning, he will learn to live with and respect decisions that he knows make you happy if he wants to be by your side. Furthermore, you want your husband to always be attracted to the woman that he sees. We are not going to be the same size our entire lives, and it is unfair for anyone to expect us to be, however, as long as you are offering the best version of you, anyone that loves you will love what they see because the care you have for yourself will only get better over time.

Don't stop getting your hair done or getting dressed up cute when you go out just because you've been together for some time and you feel like you don't have to impress him anymore. That is probably one of the most insulting to a man because you're blatantly taking his love for granted, as if he can't see any other woman but you, and that you are the only woman that he could ever have or find attractive. The same applies for him, and sometimes you have to lead by example. If you make it a point to keep yourself up you will make him more conscious of his physical presentation as well, thus keeping you both at your best and that fresh fire alive in your marriage. You are his, and he is yours, and both of you deserve to have the best version of each other as often as possible.

**Career and Lifestyle**

Last but not least, two of the most definitive influences in determining what is right for you versus what is wrong for you, are your career and your lifestyle. These two things are usually what set most women apart. There are general rules that apply to all or most when it comes to body shape and marital status, but this portion of the book is more personal.

When determining what is right and wrong for your lifestyle, you have to go deeper into who you are and what you want to represent. You have to evaluate your personal morals and standards and ask yourself "What message am I sending to other people as it pertains to my image and the way I live?" Also, you have to ask yourself "Who is watching me? Who am I trying to influence?" As a mother, a community leader, a school leader, a boss, an aunt, a big sister, or a church choir member - whatever your position maybe, you have to be ever so mindful of who is being influenced by what you do and how you carry yourself, because somebody is always watching. No, you should not live your life for other people, however, you cannot ignore the responsibility of your lifestyle. Every time you get dressed and leave the house you are sending a message about your lifestyle through your image.

You might be telling the world that you are a classy woman that takes care of herself, or you might be telling the world that you like to party hard and you had a long night last night. You might be telling the world that you are a career woman that values her professional image, or you might be telling the world that you hate your job and that you're struggling to make it. However, here is the secret: The world will only know what you let them see. When thinking about *Imaging on Purpose* be sure to tell people what you want them to know, and nothing more.

I am by no means suggesting that you lie or play make believe, but I am suggesting that you carry yourself in a way that doesn't tell all your business. The world doesn't need to know you're struggling, that you like to drink, or that you hate your job. Don't allow your life to be unnecessary entertainment. A lot of women don't care, and there is nothing that I can write in this book to make someone care. However, for those that do, make sure that your overall image fits the lifestyle that you live. It is a challenge to give general rules and assessments for lifestyle imaging because like I said, it really depends on the person. Nevertheless, be realistic, and be honest in your choosing not just things for you current lifestyle, but for the lifestyle you want to live.

Finally, let's talk about careers. Whether you love your job or hate it, it definitely plays a part in your image. When we start talking business and career, it becomes more than simply a matter of looking good and bad, it becomes a matter of branding. Your brand is likened to your credit, or your reputation. It is the things that becomes synonymous with your name; it is the thing that immediately comes to mind when people see you or hear your name. Brand is created through consistency, whether it is good or bad, intentional or unintentional.

As much as you want to be judged based off of who you are inside, and to be given opportunities to succeed based on knowledge and experience, your physical presentation has a large effect on your career and its longevity. Studies have also shown that your image has a direct effect on your pay. Your height, weight, hair color, makeup, dress, general attractiveness, and even being "too pretty" are all things that can effect potential employment, or even the receptiveness of others in the professional market.

If you base your entire existence off of others receiving you, you will struggle for the rest of your life, so I am in no way suggesting that. However, I am suggesting that you use what you've got to create what you want. Find the balance – whatever that means for you, and make sure that your image lines up with your profession, and/or your professional aspirations. Make your image work for you. LOOK like you know what you're talking about. LOOK like you have an education. LOOK like you care. Also, understand that you are a walking billboard for you and your brand, 24 hours a day, 7 days a week, 365 days of the year and 366 on a leap year. In other words, all the time.

You never know when you may come in contact with a potential employer, or when you may make a connection that could change your life. Of course performance will always take precedence over looks, but you want to make sure that the image you put forth will help you, and not hurt you. Understand that what others may wear, or how they may carry themselves may not be applicable for you and what you do. When I am doing image consultations for clients I always ask the client to pick out three words or characteristics that they want their brand to represent or to be synonymous with, and embody those characteristics in everything that they do. Even if you work a job you don't love, or one where you have to wear uniforms every day, if you want to relay zeal and vibrancy through your physical presentation, color your hair, do your makeup- use what you've got to create what you want.

There are many things about life that you cannot change, but there are just as many things that you can. Accepting who you are, what you do, what is right for you and what is wrong for you just puts you that much closer to The Upgrade.

# Chapter 3

## *Appropriate vs. Inappropriate*

In the previous chapters we discussed understanding the correlation between your image and your purpose, what is right for you versus what is wrong for you – two topics that are personal and are specifically catered to you and your lifestyle. However, when discussing what is appropriate versus what is inappropriate, there are some suggestions of a general matter that are applicable. This entire chapter is based on one principle:

There is a time and a place for everything.

Many times the message we think we are sending with our image and what is actually being communicated is totally different. The message we're sending may be inappropriate merely because of the fact that we are doing what we think is the right thing, at the wrong time. The saddest part is that people will pass judgment and talk about you based on inappropriateness, but it is rare that someone will actually confront the issue, or help you understand why what you are doing or the image you have presented is inappropriate.

My goal in this chapter is to be the one who will help you, not pass judgment on you. I will point out specific areas of inappropriateness and let you determine if they apply to you. I want you to understand what is appropriate, why, and when, so that no one will ever be able to hold that against you.

As I mentioned, you should live every day on purpose, and get dressed every day with your purpose in mind. Not only do you have to consider the bigger picture of who you are and who you want to be, but you have to consider the real and tangible aspect of the situation. Ask yourself,

- What am I doing today?
- Who will I see?
- What do I want my image to accomplish?

You may ask yourself these questions and determine that you want to look nice without considering one of the biggest issues, which is:

•   Is there anything about my physical presentation today that could potentially be considered offensive, distracting, or embarrassing?

Consider the message you send if you go to work or to an interview with your cleavage overexposed? What will happen if you go to church in a dress that is too short and accidently drop something on the ground? Before you leave home or the department store with a new garment, ask yourself; Is the material of my garment (shirt, skirt, pants) transparent? Are my undergarments visible through my clothing? Should I put on a different type/color underwear? If that question was a conscious thought on a daily basis it would keep a lot of us from walking out of the house looking the way we sometimes do. The problem with many of us is not that we don't know, it's that we don't slow down long enough to think.

### Understanding the Appropriate Time and Place

There is a secret code that we as women must learn and understand. Its concepts are essential in making your image work for you. That code is called the **Understood Dress Code - UDC** (I just made that up by the way). This code may also be referred to as Common Sense, even though its concepts don't seem to be common knowledge in this day and time. It is rare that the code is verbalized or actually written out, but most places have one - they simply expect you to use context clues and common sense to figure it out. Let's break down this code and address the general expectations of each place.

### Day Time Attire

The UDS of day attire is probably the most general. Casual dress is acceptable because most day activities are fairly lax in their requirements. Day attire is what you would wear to shop, to pick your child up from school, or even to a doctor's appointment. It is your daily default presentation when no one is giving you mandates as to how you are supposed to look that day; what you wear and how you carry yourself when you think no one is looking.

Each person has their own daily default. Who's to say whether your daily default is right or wrong? It totally depends on your personal standard. However there are three questions you need to ask yourself before you leave the house.

1) Am I covered properly?
   - Make sure that every crease, crack, and corner that should be covered is covered before you step out of your house. Make sure undergarments that are supposed to be under your clothes stay under your clothes. (There is nothing more unattractive than someone walking around with their pink-polka dotted bra hanging out of the back of their shirt!) Also, make sure that your body is covered as it should be. Save your cleavage, mid-drifts, and short skirts for the club. The day-time is not the time to be sex. Day time is the time to handle business. Keep this in mind if you want others to take you seriously.
   - In addition to making sure your clothes stay put, pay attention to the bra you wear, have appropriate underwear, and any other necessary undergarments (camisoles, girdles, etc.) - regardless of what you have on. My late grandmother once told me, "You're never too young to wear a girdle." And although I found that statement to be comical, there was so much wisdom behind it. She wasn't just talking about shape wear, she was alluding to the fact that looking sloppy will never be acceptable, no matter who you are, how old you are, where you come from or where you are going. If you can see your back fat or your gut hanging out of your clothing, so can everyone else. Be mindful of that. You don't have to get dressed from head to toe to run an errand or go to grocery store, because I sure don't. However, you never want to send an offensive message or one that says that you don't care about my body and how it is represented. Be conscious both that you are covered and of *how* you are covered.

2)  Am I clean?

  * This is major ladies. You would think that general hygiene should go without saying, especially in adults, but it doesn't so I'm saying it. Do not leave the house without making sure that your body is clean, and that you smell clean Be conscious of your bodily odors and remember that if you can smell you, so can other people. As women we sweat in some of the weirdest places, and our bodies can brew up some of the most interesting aromas, so be conscious of that. Don't act like it doesn't exist. Keep baby wipes, baby powder and perfume on hand if necessary to ensure that your scent is always pleasant. If you don't remember anything else from this book, remember this:

    You only look as good as you smell.

    Once you are clean, you also want to make sure that you look clean. Your clothes should be ironed and clean. Save your damaged sweat pants and tee shirts for a lounge day at home. Lastly, your hair should always be done. You can smell like heaven on earth and your outfit can to be fabulous as ever, but if your hair is all over our head you present an unkempt package. Even if you are in between styles or appointments, put on a hat. A grown woman should never be caught looking messy by the head!

3)  Am I ready for the world?

  * How many times have you walked out the house looking all wrong, thinking you would be out for a quick errand and right back home, only to see someone you know and either hide to keep them from seeing you, or run from embarrassment at your hair/hygiene/attire to avoid speaking? It has happened to all of us, and the first thing that we say is, "Of all the days that they could see me… they had to see me on the day that I look like crap!" We may hate it sometimes and yes, it may take a few extra minutes, but if you stay ready you will never have to get ready! You are a walking, talking, 24 hour advertisement

for your brand. You never know who you will meet, or what you will need to be ready for.

- General rule: Your physical presentation should never cause someone to question who you are, or what you do. You should never have to hand out your business card or even have a conversation with someone while simultaneously giving your disclaimer explaining why the way you look. I am by no means suggesting that you walk around with a full face of makeup and heels every day, because I don't even do that. I am merely suggesting that you be conscious of the way you look, no matter where you are going or who you think you're going to see.

**Professional Image**

Appropriate professional image largely depends on your profession. There are two standards of business attire: business professional and business casual. Business professional means suits, dresses and skirts, all of conservative length, and business casual means you can wear slacks, no jacket – it's very simple. Some professions don't have a dress code, and give more allowance to creativity and self-expression. However, there is one rule that applies to all: Your professional image should never be offensive. Excessive skin showing (cleavage, mid-section) and attire with explicit imageries, writing or messages are a few examples of things that will never be appropriate in a professional setting.

Moreover, unless you are a hairstylist or makeup artist, your makeup and hair should both be conservative and neutral. The word professional puts you in the mindset of business, which alludes to monetary exchange. Even though your image should be that of your target audience, all money is green, and you don't want to offend any potential consumers. Be sure to present a polished image that enhances your business, not hinders it. Before you open your mouth to tell someone who you are or what you do, they look at you from head to toe and decide how they feel about you based on what they see. Don't sell yourself short by turning people off before they have a chance to get to know you!

**Evening Attire**

Evening attire is not limited to things that are worn only in the evening. It also includes anything that is worn for special events or occasions. It may be as simple as what you would wear out on date, a night out with the girls, or what you might wear to a wedding or party. There is such a fine line when it comes to what is appropriate and inappropriate for night attire. Most woman want to turn it up a notch at night, and they want to be more sexy or appealing to the eye. However, how do you draw the line between sexy and inappropriate? How do you present an image that is attractive, appealing and classy? What is appropriate or inappropriate for you largely depends on where you are going, the purpose of the event or occasion, and what you want to accomplish while there. Let's look at some different scenarios.

## Semi-formal Event

Semi-formal events are the most common. They range from weekly church services, to weddings, to fundraisers, to bridal showers. Semi-formal attire is often referred to as "church clothes" or "dress clothes". This does not always mean that you are expected to wear your Easter Sunday dress. It simply implies that you are expected to get more dressed up than you usually do. Now it is important to consider the nature of an event when you are deciding on your semi-formal presentation. Understand conservative boundaries, and know that places such as church, political events, or events that are more family oriented are not the places to wear your mini-dress and your dramatic, over the top makeup. When you are going to places like that the focus should not be on you. Your skirt length should not be any higher than a couple of inches above your knee, and your body should be covered. Period. No questions asked. Anything beyond that is disrespectful.

If you have to hold your garment down in the back to bend over or if you have to put your hand over your chest to catch your breasts from falling out as you lean forward, your attire is cut too high or low respectively. This is the time to be classy and stylish, not the time to be sexy. Focus on enhancing your natural beauty; this is not the time to wear your rainbow, over the top face paint or your dramatic false lashes. If you would wear it to the club, you should never - and I mean never, wear it to church or any other conservative event.

When attending more personal events such as weddings or parties, use those times to show a little more of your personal style and flair, but even in those circumstances you need to understand that semi-formal attire has an overall conservative connotation, and that you should dress yourself accordingly.

## A Night Out/Party Attire

This is where things get tricky. Most of the time when women go out, they are either going out with someone, or going out hoping to meet someone... as in a man. Am I right or am I right? You may go out with the intention of just "having fun with the girls", but in most cases you want to mingle with the opposite sex. The desire to be found attractive causes women to go way too far and rather than looking appealing, they end up looking trashy.

My daddy used to always tell me "You have to leave something to the imagination", which is a concept that most women struggle with when it comes to these kinds of outings. Have you ever considered what types of men are attracted to women that walk about with only the bare essentials of their body covered looking like a FOR SALE sign is plastered across her backside? (That's another topic for another book.)

The key to mastering this with class is understanding the art of balance. Pick one limit, push it, and leave the rest alone. For example: If you know your dress is extremely form fitting, make sure that it is longer and covers most of your body. If you're wearing a really tight bottom, wear a loose top, or vice versa. If your makeup is over the top, wear a more conservative outfit. If you're showing a little cleavage, make sure your legs are covered. Are you catching my drift? It's ok to push the limit a little bit, but pick one and stick with it. Pushing too many limits at once always results in attire that lacks class and is unsuitable no matter what the occasion.

## Cocktail vs. Formal/Black Tie Events

The only major difference between a cocktail event and a formal is the length of your dress. A cocktail dress is a shorter version of an evening gown, but if either of these are requested for an event, know that you are supposed to dress up. There isn't much to be said concerning formal events, because this is the time to go all out. Pull out your best gown and play princess! Enjoy being a woman. Throw some curls in your hair and glam your makeup to the max. Even if you are not into makeup, no grown woman should go to a formal barefaced. This is the time to embrace your femininity have fun getting dolled-up.

Don't let your efforts to look presentable be in vain, just because you were doing what you though was the right thing at the wrong time. Think about the time, the place, who will be there, and what you want to accomplish and you will have no problem deciphering what is appropriate, and what is inappropriate.

# Chapter 4

## *The Process*

Now that you have acknowledged that you want to make a change and you understand the rules, where do you start? How do you begin The Upgrade? Whether you realize it or not, your upgrade has already begun. Changing the way you *think* is the first and most important step in changing the way you *look*. If you can do that successfully, the rest of this process will be a piece of cake. Physical changes are temporary, but a mental change will be what totally changes your life.

Any time I am doing a full makeover for a client, one of the first things I ask them is what they want to change about their look; in essence, what are you dissatisfied with? Shortly thereafter, I ask them what they want to look like. More often than not, they don't know or are not comfortable answering my questions. I challenge you to ask yourself those tough questions, and to really be honest. Just as I encourage them as I encourage you to begin with your end in mind. See yourself in the future, and believe that this life changing transformation, The Upgrade, is possible, even for you.

We have discussed who you are, where you are, and where you are going. You have an accurate perception of the woman in the mirror, so now you must set your sights on the woman that you are becoming, even as you read this book. Even if you are not totally dissatisfied with the woman that you are, you can always be better, and I hope that as you have read this book you have begun to think about the different areas in which you can improve.

Who is someone that embodies the characteristics you want to display in your physical appearance? What women do you admire or want to emulate? We spend so much time being competitive that we forget it is perfectly fine to look to other women, not for imitation, but for inspiration. It is good to use fellow sisters as our impetus or compass during our transformation process. In this day and time of high accessibility, we are constantly exposed to images of other beautiful, vibrant women; be they celebrities, or every day women like us. Social media has made it especially easy to get visual depictions of a particular life or style on a daily basis. I would urge you to use these things as resources, and not for comparison. If you take bits and pieces of those images, noticing what you like about them, and combine those things with your lifestyle and the things that make you unique, you have will have a good idea as to where to go with your image.

While copying someone else's image isn't your goal, you can use the things that you like about another's style and presentation as motivation and inspiration. It's not much different than looking in a home and garden magazine for ideas or reading a fitness book to help reach your goals. In doing this, you want to make sure that you are looking to women that live similar lifestyles that you live, or that you want to live. It may be a tad bit unrealistic for an elementary school teacher or mother of 4 to look to Beyonce' for inspiration. We all love her, but she gets paid to look the way she does, so she may not be the best point of reference. Celebrities are great, however, you can find great inspiration in the women that you see everyday. You may find inspiration in your hairstylist, your pastor's wife, a professional friend, or even a random woman you see walking through the mall. I am always looking and taking mental notes from the beautiful women I encounter on a daily basis, and there is absolutely nothing wrong with that. Again, use these women as points of inspiration, not comparison. I cannot stress that enough. Comparison is the thief of happiness and the root of low self-esteem. Allow what you see to inspire you, and help you visualize where you want to go.

Once you are able to visualize where you want to go, you can officially begin the physical process of The Upgrade.

**Start From the Top**

Don't know where to begin? Start at the top!

The top meaning your head; more specifically, your hair. Even a slight change in your hair is a quick way to totally change your look, and more importantly, how you feel about your look. Choose a style that will compliment your features and your lifestyle, and go for it! When you get tired of your look and you want a change, change it again! It's that simple.

With the options we have at our fingertips to include extensions and wigs these days, almost any hairstyle is achievable, and changeable in a snap. Why limit yourself?

I know that we are sensitive when it comes to our hair. When it's right, we are our most confident, but when it's wrong… we don't even want to be seen! Our self-esteem can take a real hit and totally goes down the drain when our hair isn't how we would like it.

The truth is you aren't going to look camera ready all of the time, but if you can make it a point to maintain your hair, it will be easier to maintain your image overall. Your hair should be a priority. No questions asked. Connect yourself to a stylist that doesn't just style your hair well, but one that can care for your hair and also keep you moving forward with your image adjustments.

There is nothing more telling than a woman who has worn her hair the exact same way for years. I don't know who's to blame: her or her beautician. Regardless, your hair is one of the first things that people notice when they see you, sometimes even before they notice your face. Make a statement with it. Keep in mind your statement can be strong and subtle. You don't have to shock the world by changing your style every week. However, small changes will keep your image fresh. That statement alone will speak volumes.

Now let's talk about your most important feature: your beautiful face!

There are thousands of companies solely dedicated to putting out products that enhance this single feature, so it must be a big deal. I wouldn't dare insist that every woman has to wear makeup every day and all the time, nor would I dare suggest that every woman shouldn't.

Makeup can be one of your greatest accessories. It's also fun. Experiment with lipsticks, glosses, and different color shades to give your look that extra oomph you've been searching for.

Makeup can completely transform a plain-Jane look into something glamorous. For those that immediately thought, *I have no idea what I'm doing* as soon as I began discussing makeup, my advice to you is: The only way to learn is by doing. Take advantage of the plethora of makeup courses offered by artists, YouTube tutorials and employees at your local cosmetic counters. Don't be intimidated by what you don't know. Be open to learn. That's what this process is all about.

**Every Woman Should Have...**

First and foremost, it is important to establish a firm foundation. There are certain things that as a woman, no matter who you are or what you do, you should own. These things are the fundamentals of creating an image that is versatile and timeless. If you invest in quality pieces, these are all things that you can keep for many years to come.

1) The standard black dress: Your standard black dress will probably be one of the most frequently worn pieces in your closet, because it is so versatile. It is best of this dress is plain, and short or cap-sleeved so that it can be worn year round. You can add a blazer or cardigan and wear it in semi-formal or professional environments, or you can add a nice chunky necklace to jazz is up for a formal event. It is best if you invest in quality fabric, not something that will stretch or fade. Dry clean it to ensure that you get the maximum wear out of your dress.

2) The multi-purpose black suit: The black suit, much like the standard black dress, is the gift that will keep on giving. If you are fortunate enough to score a black suit that has both pants and a skirt, you will be able to light two candles with one flame. With a black blazer, a black skirt, and a pair of black slacks you now have all the fundamental pieces of a woman's closet. Whether you need to attend a memorial, professional event or a job interview, your black suit will never let you down.

3) Power pumps: Every woman must have a good pair of black pumps, and at least one other neutral color; latte or espresso colors are great. If you have both of these, you will never have to worry about not having shoes to wear with any given color.

4) Essential whites: A white button-down shirt, a plain white cotton tee, and a plain white camisole - these are your essential whites. They can be worn by themselves or as part

of a layered ensemble. It would be a plus to have these same pieces in black.

5) A pair of dark-washed jeans: You don't have to have 20 pairs of jeans, all you really need is one *nice* pair of jeans. A dark wash is more versatile than a light wash because it can be dressed up or down. Avoid distressing and pocket embroidery for your standard pair. Keep it simple. Versatility is key.

Have you noticed a recurring theme with these *must haves*? They are all classic pieces in neutral colors. Other standard pieces like leggings, cardigans, boots, flats, quality handbags and underwear in neutral colors like oatmeal, caramel, and grey can also be added to this list.

**Beauty Must-Haves**

If you haven't figured it out by now, I am pro-woman and pro-femininity! We are naturally beautiful creatures, and we should embrace products that are made to enhance that beauty. Many women are turned off by the inappropriate use of these products, but don't let other people's ignorance drive you away. Beauty products are your friend! Even if you don't want to wear a full face of makeup, every woman should at least have mascara, and some lip-gloss.

You would be surprised at how those simple products can enhance your face. For those that do want to venture into Glam-land, you can start off with the basics: foundation, concealer, setting powder, blush, eyeliner, and a pallet of neutral eye shadow colors. These items will take you a long way in Glam-land! Also, take advantage off all of the sweet scents and perfumes that are available to you. As I said before, you only look as good as you smell. Isn't it interesting how something invisible can have such an impact on your overall image? Attract them with your beauty, then, entice them with your lovely smell.

**Make a Statement**

Once you have purchased your essentials, you can begin to add more colorful and stylish pieces to give you a unique and stylish edge. Try to have a statement piece or a focal point in every outfit.

A focal point is not just limited to something that you wear - it can be your hair, nails, makeup, or accessories. This is what separates the plain-Jane's from the Divas. Use simple things to accentuate your look. You would be surprised at how some fun lipstick or a few curls in your hair can add to your look. Also, using odd or unpredictable color combinations can add an extra edge. Honestly, you can wear a trash bag and be fabulous if you do it with confidence. Here's my point: If you believe you look good, other people will to! While wearing a trash bag isn't recommended, I do want you to take calculated fashion risks you might not normally take. Remember, this book is entitled The Upgrade!

The more risks you take, the more comfortable you will become taking those risks. The more comfortable you become, the better you'll feel about your new, upgraded you! As you see what works for your style/purpose/image, you can begin to develop your signature look. Your signature might be your edgy haircut, your charming prescription frames, or even your love for mixing funky patterns. Whatever it may be, own it undeniably. It can save you, no matter how you look. I personally love designer handbags, so even on my worst day, my handbag is going to tell you a lot about who I am. That is the point of having a *signature*; you won't have to say a word - it will speak for you. You want your personality to show through your appearance!

Many women avoid this very principle, because they don't want to stand out. Rather than making a statement, they choose to blend in with the crowd so that they don't draw attention to themselves. However I'm not sure what's worse, getting too much attention or not getting any attention at all. We all desire attention of some sort, whether we want to admit it or not. At some point we want to know that someone thinks we look nice, or that the image we are presenting is enhancing our business. There is absolutely nothing wrong with that. It is important that we are attracting the right kind of attention, at the right time. You deserve a word of encouragement or a pat on the back every now and then. At least I think so. Embrace and love who you are so that others can embrace and love you as well.

# Chapter 5

## *Seal The Deal*

I can remember the day like it was yesterday. It had been a long day and I was finishing up my last client. At the time I was still in school, hustling and swinging weaves out of my one-bedroom apartment. It was the first time that this particular girl had come to me to get her hair done, and we were trying something different. After I finished her sophisticated-bob-cut-sew-in, she got up and went into the bathroom to see the finished product. Shortly thereafter, I heard a loud gasp, followed by some screams. I rushed to the bathroom to see what was wrong. I thought she had hurt herself or worse, that she hated her hairdo. I was met by a young woman with tears in her eyes. All she could say to me was "I have never looked like this in my life..."

In that moment I realized I was on to something. I understood that the gift that was inside of me was much bigger than just making someone's hair look different, or doing their makeup for an event. It was much deeper just than helping someone choose a new outfit. It was more than just a hustle. I was indeed on a mission.

From that point forward, I dedicated my life to seeing that very reaction. I wanted all of my clients to be more confident and more excited about the way they looked. Rather than simply giving people what they asked for and taking their money, I decided to take a more personal approach. I began to look at the person that was inside, their lifestyle, and the things that were important to them. It was only when I grasped their persona that I would make suggestions that would allow their inner person to resonate on the outside. When I changed my focus, I immediately saw a shift in my business and like driving out of gloomy fog into the sun, my purpose became much clearer.

&) CR

Women carry so much. As if our own insecurities and worries aren't enough, oftentimes we carry the issues of the people around us and it can cause us to neglect ourselves. If you don't take anything else from this book, I want you to know that no matter what you are going through or what has happened to you, you are beautifully, fearfully, and wonderfully made. Don't allow the circumstances of life to rob you of your essence. You are a glorious woman, and you are phenomenal!

I challenge you to begin to make a change today. It doesn't take a lot of money or time; just some effort and a made up mind. Let today be the last day you bristly walk past a mirror and avoid looking at yourself because you don't like what you see. Let today be the last day that you allow your low self-esteem to effect your relationships and the way you communicate. Let today be the last day that you allow your image to hinder you reaching your goals. Whether it be something as drastic as throwing out your current wardrobe, or something as simple as just putting on some lip gloss, you can immediately begin to make a change. The journey of a thousand miles begins with one step, and you can take that step today.

Enjoy this process. Fall in love with the woman you are, and the woman you are becoming. Accept your flaws and imperfections, but love yourself enough to not be languid or complacent about being your best self. Commit yourself to becoming a better woman, and being the best you can possibly be. Consequently, you entire quality of life will improve. Your daily disposition will be totally different, and your self-esteem will improve. As a result, your relationships and the way you interact with other people will follow suit. Because you made the decision to use The Upgrade, your image will develop, consequently upgrading your entire life.

Congratulations! I'm proud of you for being willing to make this change. It might come as a surprise, but my passion does not live in hair, makeup, or fashion. I am passionate about TRANSFORMATION. I am smitten with the overall idea of women being the absolute best we can be. I understand that there is a direct correlation between the way a woman looks and how she feels. I know that if a woman has the courage to face and conquer her inner obstacles, nothing can stop her from being successful.

My honest desire for you and every woman that will read this book is to be empowered, inspired, motivated, and ultimately transformed. There is nothing more commanding than a woman who is confident, purpose driven, and committed to being the best she can be. The only thing standing in the way of you becoming the woman that you have always wanted to be is YOU. Don't allow fear of something new or the lack of confidence to keep you where you are. You aren't comfortable here, so it's time to move forward. You have what it takes, now the rest is up to you! Take that leap of faith, and create the image and life that you want. You're a diamond in the rough, and I can't wait to see you shine!

YOU HAVE OFFICIALLY BEEN UPGRADED
J.Renee
11/20/2013 12:19 AM

# About The Author

Inspiration, transformation, and motivation are the three principles that guide and shape the essence of J. Renee. A native of Clarksville, Tennessee, J.Renee is the president and CEO of ALL THINGS J.RENEE INC. As a widely sought-after beauty industry professional, motivational, and keynote speaker and businesswoman, she is passionate about developing others and is very intentional and strategic about her pursuits.

While overcoming various life obstacles, she has defied the odds and risen above the expectations levied upon her by circumstance. Consequently, she has made it her life mission to inspire others to be the best that they can be. As an accomplished hairstylist and makeup artist, she specializes in aiding in the transformation of women, not just externally, but also internally. Such a desire has led her to author her first book entitled "The Upgrade."

As a businesswoman, she takes great pride in establishing a legacy of excellence so that generations to come will know the profound impact she has had on society. She is the owner of an online store, Shop All Things J.Renee, as well as an extension hairline, The J.Renee Signature Hair Collection. As a motivator, she is a mentor and founder of the I'm Every Woman Mentoring Program, and a speaker who compels her listeners to action, thus causing them to go to the next level in their life.

Her personal philosophy is that there is no point in taking potential to the grave; when she dies, she wants to be all used up, and she wants every person she is connected to, to be used up as well.

Printed in the United States
By Bookmasters